But I was free, and they should be free.
-Harriet Tubman

I am not afraid... I was born to do this
-Joan of Arc

I am a queen. And as long as I live, I will reign.
-Zenobia

To create one's world in any of the arts takes courage.
-Georgia O'Keeffe

...a Woodhull

side of the room and the guys on the other side of the room. I guess they didn't want to associate with me. But I could hold my own with them and sometimes did better. -Mary Golda Ross

A woman is like a tea bag. You can't tell how strong she is until you put her in hot water.
-Eleanor Roosevelt

HISTORY'S YEARBOOK

VIRGINIA LOH-HAGAN

GIRL WARRIORS

The world has used me so unkindly. I fear it has made me suspicious of everyone.
-Mary Anning

Liberty!
–Inayat Khan's last word

If you hold your hand closed, nothing good can come in. The open hand is blessed, for it gives in abundance, even as it receives. -Biddy Mason

I've never been afraid in my life.
-Nancy Wake

I attribute my success to this: I never gave or took any excuse.
-Florence Nightingale

Women should be someone, and not something.
–Mary Cassatt

Well-behaved women seldom make history.
-Laurel Thatcher Ulrich

Here is the day. We must welcome it with song.
–Marie Laveau

The title of Queen rang sweet to my ears.
-Catherine the Great

I0896420

Contents

Introduction

We are celebrating girl **warriors**! Warriors are fighters. They serve in the military. They fight in wars. They stand up against evil. They overcome challenges. Challenges are hard tasks.

It's not easy being a girl warrior. Many people think that women shouldn't fight. Women weren't allowed to be soldiers. They weren't allowed to be on the battlefields. Laws have changed. Women can now serve. Why did it take so long?

Throughout history, women have shown that they're tough. They're brave. They're strong. The girl warriors in this book rise to the top. They paved the way for today's girl warriors. You don't have to be in a real battle to be a warrior. If you are confident and compassionate, you're a warrior. If you stand up for what's right, you're a warrior.

Here's to you and all the girl warriors in our lives!

chapter 1

BEST ALL-AROUND

Dahomey Amazons

The blood flows. You are dead.
The blood flows. We have won!

– A song of victory and dance sung by some Dahomey Amazons

The "Best All-Around" award goes to the Dahomey Amazons! Amazons were from Greek myths. They're a group of fierce girl warriors. Dahomey is now called Benin. Benin is a country in West Africa.

Thousands of Dahomey women served together. They trained to protect their king and kill others. They were an **elite** fighting force. Elite means the best.

The Dahomey Amazons started in the 1700s. They served for almost 200 years. A bell was rung when they left the king's castle. This was a warning. Men were to get out of their way. They were to look away. Touching these women meant death.

chapter 2

LEADER OF THE PACK

Maria Bochkareva

> I want women whose hearts are pure crystal, whose souls are pure, whose impulses are lofty. With such women setting an example of self-sacrifice, you men will realize your duty in this grave hour.
>
> –Maria Bochkareva

The "Leader of the Pack" award goes to Maria Bochkareva. Bochkareva lived from 1889 to 1920. She had a rough life. But she never quit. She became a Russian soldier. She fought in World War I. She was the first Russian woman to command a military unit. She formed the "Women's **Battalion** of Death." Battalions are troops ready for battle. She did this in 1917.

Bochkareva's all-women army was strong. She trained about 2,000 women. She was a tough leader. Only 300 women passed training. Bochkareva's battalion fought against the Germans. They fought next to an all-male army. The men didn't want to leave their area. The women did. They fought on the battlefields. They did what men were afraid to do.

chapter 3

MOST PERSISTENT

Nakano Takeko

I was determined to fight, for I have the skills and knowledge, which I was going to put to use.

–Nakano Takeko

The "Most **Persistent**" award goes to Nakano Takeko. Persistent means not quitting. Takeko didn't take "no" for an answer. Women were denied education. They were denied rights. They couldn't join the army.

Takeko didn't care. She became a **samurai**. A samurai is a Japanese warrior. Takeko was one of the few females to do this. She trained in the **martial arts**. Martial arts are special fighting skills. She created her own women's army. She fought in the Boshin War. This war was from 1868 to 1869.

Takeko got shot in the chest. She didn't want her enemy to have her body. So, she had her sister cut off her head. Her sister buried her head under a pine tree. Takeko is still making her mark. Every year, girls go to her pine tree. They honor her.

chapter 4

MOST ATHLETIC

Khutulun

> [Khutulun fought] as deftly as a hawk pounces on a bird.
>
> –Marco Polo, Italian explorer and writer

The "Most Athletic" award goes to Khutulun. Khutulun was known as the "wrestler princess." She competed in many wrestling contests. She beat every man. She said she'd only marry a man who could beat her. Losers had to give her horses. She won a lot. So, she had a lot of horses.

She was good at many sports. She was a good horse rider.

She was an archer. Archers shoot with a bow and arrows. Khutulun was also good at fighting in wars. She was born in 1260. Her family was the Khans. They ruled Mongolia for years. They were tough fighters. Khutulun fought with her father and brothers. She was every bit as fierce as them.

chapter 5

MOST LOYAL

Mai Bhago

> Everybody has to die. Why not die like a brave person? If you don't join me, I shall take a party of women and die for the guru.
>
> –Mai Bhago

The "Most Loyal" award goes to Mai Bhago. Bhago was very loyal to the Sikh **guru** Gobind Singh. Gurus in the Sikh religion are holy people. Singh was in a battle in 1705. Forty men left him. This means they ran away from military service.

Bhago was mad. She found the 40 men. She made them return to Singh. She made them say they were sorry.

She led the men in battle. She and the men fought. Almost all of them died. Bhago was hurt. But she survived. Singh took care of her. Bhago lived with Singh. She became his bodyguard. She dressed like a man.

chapter 6

BEST TEAM PLAYER

Zenobia

> I am a queen. And as long as I live, I will reign.
>
> –Zenobia

The "Best Team Player" award goes to Zenobia. Zenobia's husband and stepson were killed. Because of this, she became queen. She ruled over Syria. She grew her empire. She invaded Egypt and other areas. She took over trade **routes**. Routes are paths.

Zenobia was known as a warrior queen. She was a good horse rider. But she liked to walk with her soldiers. She walked many miles with them. She hunted with them. She drank with them. Zenobia showed she was one of them.

There are stories that claim Rome invaded. Zenobia fought back. But she lost. She was captured. She was bound in golden chains. She died around 274 CE.

chapter 7

BEST GEAR

Trieu Thi Trinh

> I only want to ride the wind, walk the waves, slay sharks.
>
> –Trieu Thi Trinh

The "Best **Gear**" award goes to Lady Trieu Thi Trinh. Gear is necessary items used for something. Trinh was a Vietnamese warrior. She was fierce on the battlefields. It wasn't just her skills that stood out. What she wore stood out too. She wore gold **armor**. Armor is metal covering that protects the body. She wore a gold pin in her hair. She wore bright yellow robes. She wore ivory shoes. She carried a sword in each hand. She rode an elephant.

She led an army of 1,000 men. She did this at age 20. She fought against the Chinese. Chinese troops invaded Vietnam. They killed over 10,000 Vietnamese. This happened in the 3rd century.

Trinh's brother wanted her to get married. She told him, "I will not bow my head."

chapter 8

MOST PERSUASIVE

Grace O'Malley

> Take this from unconsecrated hands.
>
> –Grace O'Malley

The "Most **Persuasive**" award goes to Grace O'Malley. Persuasive means able to convince. O'Malley was called "the girl with the **cropped** hair." Cropped means cut. O'Malley had long red hair. When she was young, she wanted to go sailing. Her father didn't let girls sail. He said her long hair would get caught in the ropes. O'Malley didn't accept this. She chopped off her hair. She learned to sail.

She lived in the 16th century. She was Irish. She was known as a pirate queen. Pirates attack and rob ships. They do this while at sea.

O'Malley ruled the seas. She was tough. She gave birth to her son on her ship. Right after, she fought invaders. She kicked them off her ship.

chapter 9

BIGGEST REBEL

Joan of Arc

I am not afraid ...
I was born to do this.

–Joan of Arc

The "Biggest Rebel" award goes to Joan of Arc. Joan was born in 1412. She is a **saint**. Saints are holy people. She did her own thing. She didn't let others tell her what to do. For example, she defied her parents. They wanted her to get married at 16. She refused. She convinced a powerful man she could win the war. The man believed her. His advisers didn't. But Joan proved them wrong. She led the French army. She fought against the English. She won. She helped make that man a king. She did this at age 18.

She cut her hair. She dressed like a man. She was jailed. She was burned at the stake. She was punished for being different.

chapter 10

DYNAMIC DUO

Dandara and Zumbi of Palmares

Black awareness means having eyes open for diversity.

–UNESCO Office in Brazil

The "**Dynamic** Duo" award goes to Dandara and Zumbi. Dynamic means energetic and good at getting things done. Dandara and her husband, Zumbi, were from Palmares. Palmares was a city of escaped slaves. Slaves ran away from farms. They went to Palmares. Dandara and Zumbi ruled Palmares.

They were warriors. They trained in capoeira. Capoeira is a martial art. It has dance and music. It's powerful. It's fast.

Dandara and Zumbi fought together. They defended their city. They freed slaves.

They fought against slavery. In 1678, a law was signed. This law made Palmares return slaves. Dandara and Zumbi didn't agree. They took command. Dandara chose death over being enslaved.

chapter 11

BRAVEST

Deborah Sampson

> Why can I not fight for my country too?
>
> –Deborah Sampson

The "Bravest" award goes to Deborah Sampson. Sampson was the first female American solider. But people thought she was a man. She tried to join the army twice. First, she pretended to be "Timothy Thayer." She didn't show up to fight. She was found out. The second time, she called herself "Robert Shurtleff." This was her dead brother's name.

She fought in the American Revolution. She served for 3 years. She got a cut on her head. She was also shot in the leg. But she took the bullet out herself. She didn't want a doctor to learn she was a woman.

She got really sick. She was taken to the hospital. That's how she was found out.

chapter

12

KINDEST

Lozen

> Lozen is my right hand... strong as a man, braver than most, and cunning in strategy. Lozen is a shield to her people. –Victorio

The "Kindest" award goes to Lozen. Lozen was an Apache warrior. The U.S. government forced her people to move to Arizona. The place was called "Hell's Forty Acres." Acres are units of land.

Victorio was Lozen's brother. He fought back. He led his own army. He attacked the people who kicked him off his lands. Lozen also fought. She rode, shot, and fought just as well as her brother.

Lozen felt sorry for the Apache women and children. They were scared to continue the journey. She led them to safety.

She couldn't keep her brother safe. Victorio died in battle. Lozen was helping a new mother and baby. When she found out, she got mad. She continued Victorio's fights. She had a special skill. She knew her enemies' movements.

Advice from the Field

Major General Marcelite J. Harris lived from 1943 to 2018. As major general, she was the highest-ranking female officer in the Air Force. She was the nation's highest-ranking African American woman in the Department of Defense. She was the first African American female to achieve such ranks. In 2010, she received the Trailblazer Award from the Black Girls Rock Foundation. She said, "I've prepared myself by looking at what it took to be outstanding and to be excellent in that area. I never thought about being a general. I just wanted to be good ... For being a trailblazer, get educated. Be determined. Be persistent. Have the dream and a goal ... Life may knock you down. But you have to choose to get yourself up. Get yourself up. Wipe yourself off. And let's get going again ... Like what you're doing. Don't try to be a special person. You are a special person."

Top Memories

- **6th Century:** "The Ballad of Mulan" was first composed. This poem tells the story of Hua Mulan. Mulan was a legendary Chinese woman warrior. She disguised herself as a man. She took her father's place in the army. She fought for 12 years. She was a great soldier. This story has inspired many girl warriors.
- **June 12, 1948:** President Harry Truman signed the Women's Armed Services Integration Act. This law allowed women to serve as full members of the U.S. armed forces. But women still couldn't serve in combat. And women could only make up 2 percent of each of the armed forces.
- **February 20, 1989:** The Canadian Human Rights Tribunal is a special group. It ordered Canadian forces to be open to women within 10 years.
- **March 9, 2015:** Gina Reque Teran became Bolivia's first female general in the military. She's the first woman in Latin America to be in charge of combat troops.

Student Life & Clubs

Are you interested in being a warrior? Consider the Junior Reserve Officers' Training Corps (JROTC). The U.S. armed forces sponsors this program. They pay for uniforms, equipment, etc. Most high schools offer JROTC. Some middle schools offer it. JROTC teachers are active or retired military members. Participants are called cadets. They develop military skills. They work in teams. They have opportunities to lead. The main goals are citizenship, leadership, character, and community service. Cadets don't have to join the military. But if they were interested, JROTC would help cadets pursue military careers. About 30 to 50 percent of the cadets join the military. Shelbi Davis is in JROTC. She said, "JROTC is based on leadership. It just helps you work with others and be able to clearly express yourself and not be afraid of what people think of you."

"Well-behaved women seldom make history."

–Laurel Thatcher Ulrich

Did You Know...

- Shield-maidens were female Vikings. They dressed like men. They fought in wars. They're in old Norse legends.
- There may have been female gladiators. Gladiators were trained fighters in ancient Rome. They fought to the death. A female gladiator is called a gladiatrix.
- Invicta Fighting Championships is the world's largest all-women's mixed martial arts organization. It was founded in 2012. Women can compete on a regular basis.

Learn More!

Atwood, Kathryn J. *Women Heroes of World War I: 16 Remarkable Resisters, Soldiers, Spies, and Medics*. Chicago: Chicago Review Press, 2014.

Atwood, Kathryn J. *Women Heroes of World War II: 26 Stories of Espionage, Sabotage, Resistance, and Rescue*. Chicago: Chicago Review Press, 2011.

Casey, Susan. *Women Heroes of the American Revolution: 20 Stories of Espionage, Sabotage, Defiance, and Rescue*. Chicago: Chicago Review Press, 2015.

Simons, Lisa M. Bolt. *Women in Combat: Bringing the Fight to the Front Lines*. North Mankato, MN: Capstone Press, 2017.

Your Turn!

Now, it's your turn!
You get to choose the
"Top of the Class: Girl
Warrior" winner.
Who would you pick?

TOP OF THE CLASS: GIRL WARRIOR

"Top of the Class" means being the best of the best. These prompts will help you think about who'd you pick for the "Top of the Class: Girl Warrior" award:

- Why is this person the best "girl warrior"? List reasons why this person deserves this award more than others.
- Think about how this person is different from girl warriors in this book. What is special about this person?
- How is this person similar to girl warriors in this book? Describe the qualities that girl warriors should have. How does this person represent those qualities?
- How does this person make the world a better place? How does this person change history? Why should we remember this person?
- Girl warriors often struggle. They may also face barriers. They're often told they can't do something. They don't run away when things get hard. How does this person overcome challenges?
- Heroes stand up for what is right. Heroes help others. How is this person a hero?
- Girl warriors defend. They fight. How is this person a fighter? What does this person fight for?
- How is this person a leader? How does this person help others be their best?

Consider This!

TAKE A POSITION! In the United States, women weren't allowed to serve in combat roles until January 2016. In 2017, for the first time, two women joined the Navy SEALs. Do you think women should be in special operations forces? Argue your point with reasons and evidence.

SAY WHAT? What do all these girl warriors have in common? Describe the challenges faced by girl warriors. Explain how these challenges are different from those faced by men.

THINK ABOUT IT! When people think of war, they think of men. Why is that? What types of roles do women usually take in wartimes?

Glossary

armor (AHR-mur) metal covering that protects the body

battalion (buh-TAL-yuhn) army of troops ready for battle

cropped (KRAHPD) cut short

dynamic (dye-NAM-ik) energetic and good at getting things done

elite (ih-LEET) top of the class, the best

gear (GEER) equipment

guru (GOO-roo) holy people in the Sikh religion

martial arts (MAHR-shuhl AHRTS) special fighting skills

persistent (pur-SIS-tuhnt) not willing to quit

persuasive (pur-SWAY-siv) convincing

routes (ROOTS) paths

saint (SAYNT) a very holy person

samurai (SAM-uh-rye) Japanese warrior

warriors (WOR-ee-urz) fighters

Index

45th Parallel Press

Published in the United States of America by Cherry Lake Publishing
Ann Arbor, Michigan
www.cherrylakepublishing.com

Reading Adviser: Marla Conn, MS, Ed., Literacy specialist, Read-Ability, Inc.
Book Designer: Jen Wahi

Photo Credits: ©Science History Images/Alamy Stock Photo, cover (left), 14; © Military PCF/Alamy Stock Photo, cover (middle), 8; ©Bain News Service, publisher/Library of Congress/Reproduction No., LC-DIG-ggbain-26862, cover (right), 6; ©Album/Alamy Stock Photo, 4; ©Rawpixel.com/Shutterstock, 10; ©A Sharma/Shutterstock, 12; ©quangpraha/iStock, 16; ©Steve Davey Photography/Alamy Stock Photo, 18; ©Morphart Creation/Shutterstock, 20; ©Marzolino/Shutterstock, 22; ©Science History Images / Alamy Stock Photo, 24; ©Shutter Fairy/Shutterstock, 26; various art pieces throughout courtesy of Shutterstock

45th Parallel Press is an imprint of Cherry Lake Publishing.

Library of Congress Cataloging-in-Publication Data

Names: Loh-Hagan, Virginia, author.
Title: Girl warriors / by Virginia Loh-Hagan.
Description: [Ann Arbor : Cherry Lake Publishing, 2019] | Series: History's yearbook | Audience: Grades: 4 to 6. | Includes bibliographical references and index.
Identifiers: LCCN 2019004196| ISBN 9781534147874 (hardcover) | ISBN 9781534150737 (pbk.) | ISBN 9781534149304 (PDF) | ISBN 9781534152168 (hosted ebook)
Subjects: LCSH: Women soldiers--Biography--Juvenile literature. | Women and war--History--Juvenile literature. | Women heroes--Biography--Juvenile literature.
Classification: LCC UB416 .L64 2019 | DDC 355.0092/52--dc23
LC record available at https://lccn.loc.gov/2019004196

Printed in the United States of America
Corporate Graphics

About the Author:

Dr. Virginia Loh-Hagan is an author, university professor, former classroom teacher, and curriculum designer. She dedicates this to all her female friends who have served or currently serve in the armed forces. She lives in San Diego with her very tall husband and very naughty dogs. To learn more about her, visit www.virginialoh.com.